North Star

North Star

written by Shelley Jinks Johnson

illustrated by Jerry Havens

Copyright © 2024 by Shelley Jinks Johnson

All rights reserved.

No part of this book (text or illustration) may be reproduced without written permission from the publisher.

Printed in the United States of America

ISBN: 979-8-9884546-2-5

This book is a project of Poetry AEX

for
Graham & George

Christmas bells and falling leaves,

No snow will grace our yards.

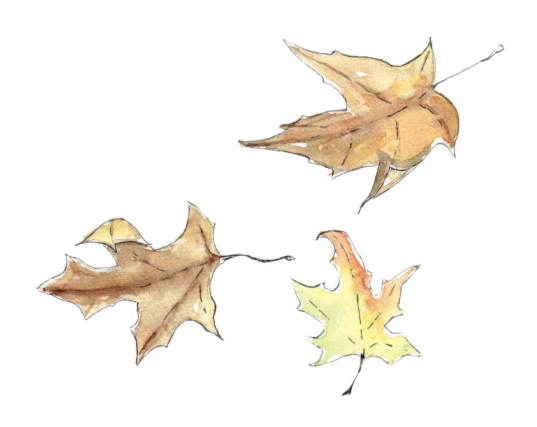

Ornaments on family trees

with happy,

festive cards.

Despite the glitter show.

Loved ones lost

we'll miss, we fear

New days they'll never know.

Still we try

to bend God's ear

to give us

one more sign.

reminding us

to shine.

For in us

Everyone,

there is a light

that lives.

and glows softly
when times are dim.

But to each

of us we can

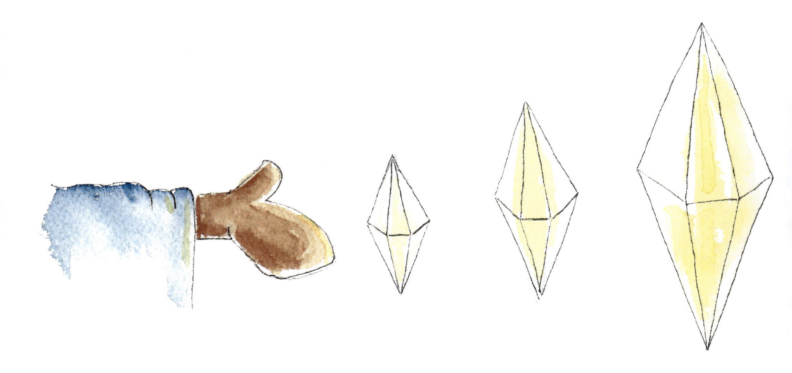

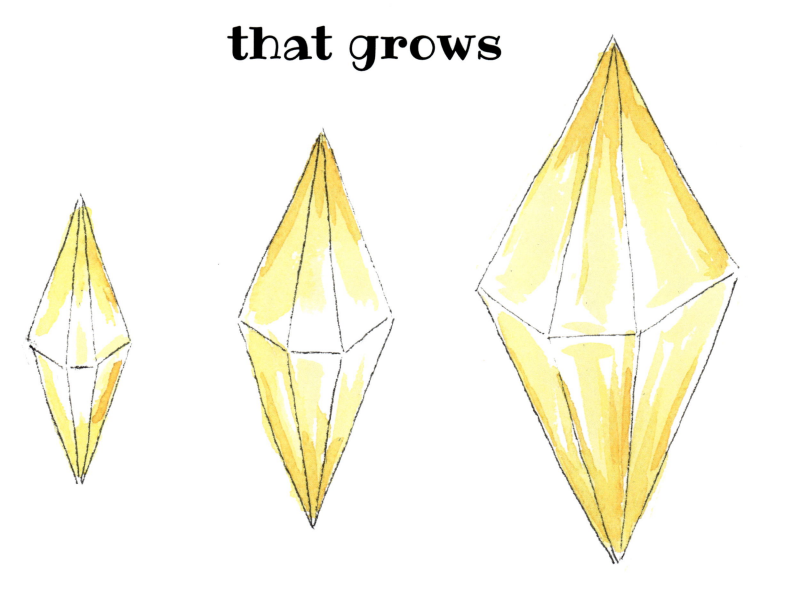

Take a hand,

one to one and

let those lights

　　　　　shine through.

Grace our world

with just a touch

of the brilliance

of

YOU!

Sing along song

There's a light in you
There's a light in me
If we join together
Then I think we will see

Love burning strong
Love burning bright
Lighting our way
Through the darkest night

I'll shine for you
And you shine for me
We'll live together
In peaceful harmony

Shelley Jinks Johnson, Author

Shelley is a poet, entrepreneur, performer, and author from Alexandria, Louisiana. In 2022 she founded Poetry AEX and was a contributor at the prestigious Bread Loaf Writer's Conference in Vermont. Co-founder of the Bad Gnus Poets writing group, she has developed her craft through various workshops and submitting her work to critical peer review. Her first collection of poetry Pretty Little Widow was published May 2023. "North Star" is her first children's book.

 @prettylittlewidow   shelleyjinksjohnson.com

Jerry Havens, Illustrator

Havens has been involved in the arts for quite a while, beginning with voice acting in commercials during his time as a local DJ/radio host. He later moved into television as a videographer and subsequently into theatre acting for almost every theatre group in central Louisiana. As a member of the Alexandria Museum of Art, he attended a family watercolor art class where he found inspiration for his future works. Briefly dabbling in oils and acrylics proved that his passion remained in watercolor as "it just moves right".

 @LAWatercolorist   Facebook.com/jerry.havens.3

Made in the USA
Coppell, TX
21 November 2024